Travel Guide To Cascais 2023

Discover the Enchanting Charms of Cascais:
A Comprehensive Travel Guide for 2023

Anthony L. Mark

Table Of Contents

INTRODUCTION

Welcome to Cascais

Cascais is a fascinating and alluring place that offers the ideal fusion of natural beauty, cultural richness, and exciting activities. It is situated along the breathtaking Portuguese coastline.

Cascais offers something for everyone, whether you're looking for white sand beaches, historical sites, outdoor activities, or simply enjoying regional food.

We cordially encourage you to go around the alluring charms of Cascais using this thorough travel guide as your guide. We hope to give you all the necessary information and insider recommendations to make your visit unforgettable in 2023 using the most recent data available.

Why Go to Cascais 2023?

Destinations like Cascais continue to draw tourists from all over the world. With new attractions, festivals, and exciting events set to take place in 2023, there will be even more reasons to visit.

Cascais guarantees a great experience whether you're a history buff, a nature lover, an adventure seeker, or a culture vulture.

Use of This Guide

To make the most of your trip to Cascais in 2023, use this guide. It is segmented into different sections that address various facets of your trip, such as preparation, sightseeing, activities, useful information, and more. You are welcome to read the entire guide or just the chapters that most appeal to you to gain a thorough understanding of Cascais.

Let this guide be your dependable travel companion as you explore Cascais' lovely streets, savour delectable cuisine, laze on immaculate beaches, and learn about its fascinating history and culture.

Prepare yourself for a once-in-a-lifetime experience in Cascais in 2023!

GETTING TO KNOW CASCAIS

History and Culture of Cascais

Cascais's geography and strategic importance as a Portuguese coastal town are intricately entwined with its history and culture. Let's explore the fascinating background behind Cascais.

1. **Overview of the past:** Cascais has a lengthy past that goes back thousands of years. Numerous civilizations, including the Phoenicians, Romans, Moors, and Christians, lived in the area. Throughout history, it served as both an important harbour and a fishing community.

2. King Louis I of Portugal made Cascais his summer home in the 19th century, which helped the city achieve

notoriety. Due to its royal ties, Cascais became a popular destination for aristocrats and nobility. The construction of grand mansions and exquisite gardens had a lasting impression on the town's architecture.

3. **Fishing village to tourist destination:** Cascais underwent a tremendous expansion and transformation in the early 20th century as a result of the expanding tourism sector.

   It became much easier to visit the town after the construction of the railway line from Lisbon to Cascais in 1889, which made it a well-liked vacation spot for both Portuguese and foreign visitors.

4. **Cultural Heritage:** The historic structures, museums, and cultural institutions of Cascais are evidence of

the city's rich cultural heritage. A remarkable collection of artwork and antiques may be seen at the Museu Condes de Castro Guimarães, which is housed in a lovely palace. The famed Portuguese artist Paula Rego's works are the focus of the Casa das Histórias Paula Rego, a one-of-a-kind museum.

5. **Events & Festivals**: Throughout the year, Cascais holds a wide range of cultural events and festivals that provide guests the chance to become immersed in the customs and festivities of the region.

Live music performances, fireworks displays, and a fun atmosphere along the waterfront are all part of the August festival known as the Festas do Mar. Music fans can experience a dynamic cultural scene at the Cascais Jazz Club and other music events.

6. **Gastronomy**: Cascais' gastronomic scene is a lovely representation of Portuguese cuisine. Fresh fish, such as sardines and codfish, as well as regional delicacies like cataplana (seafood stew) and pastéis de nata (custard tarts), take centre stage.

Don't pass up the chance to try some of the regional wines, like the well-known Vinho Verde and Port varieties.

Today, Cascais successfully combines its historic allure with contemporary comforts to create a resort that attracts a variety of tourists. It is a must-visit location for people looking for an engaging vacation experience due to its rich cultural past, breathtaking coastline vistas, and friendly attitude.

Geographical Overview

Portugal's westernmost city of Cascais is situated about 30 kilometres (18.6 miles) west of Lisbon, the nation's capital. Cascais, which is a part of the Lisbon District, is strategically located along the Portuguese Riviera's Estoril Coast.

1. **Beaches and Coastline**: The town of Cascais is fortunate to have a scenic coastline that runs for several kilometres. It is known for its stunning sandy beaches, granite cliffs, and clean waters.

   Among the most well-liked beaches in the region, Praia da Rainha, Praia da Conceição, and Praia do Guincho provide chances for swimming, sunbathing, and a variety of water activities.

2. The Sintra-Cascais Natural Park is a protected region with remarkable natural beauty and is located to the north of Cascais. This park features a variety of scenery, such as craggy mountains, dense woods, and breathtaking coastline cliffs.

   In addition to various historical landmarks including the well-known Pena Palace and the Moorish Castle, it is home to unusual flora and fauna.

3. The westernmost point of continental Europe, Cabo da Roca, is only a short distance from Cascais. Cabo da Roca is a well-known destination for travellers looking for a spectacular natural environment since it is perched on the imposing cliffs overlooking the Atlantic Ocean and offers breathtaking panoramic views.

4. **Serra de Sintra:** The Serra de Sintra mountain range rises to the northeast of Cascais, enhancing the natural splendour of the area. The mountains are dotted with attractive communities, like Sintra, a UNESCO World Heritage site renowned for its romantic palaces and enchanting ambiance, and they are covered in thick greenery.

5. **Lisbon accessibility:** Cascais has excellent access to the Portuguese capital city. Train travel between Lisbon and Cascais is simple, and the route follows a beautiful coastal path that offers breathtaking views along the way. Due to Lisbon's proximity, guests may easily tour both urban and seaside sites while they're there.

6. **Mild Climate:** The Mediterranean region of Cascais has mild winters and

balmy summers. From 8°C (46°F) in the winter to 28°C (82°F) in the summer, are the typical temperatures. The area enjoys a relaxing sea wind, which makes it a great place for beach relaxation and outdoor sports.

Cascais's geographic setting, which includes its proximity to the coast, mountains, and historical sites, provides visitors with a wide variety of experiences.

The geographic environment of Cascais makes for an enthralling backdrop for your tour, whether you're looking for beach activities, nature discovery, or cultural immersion.

Climate and Best Time to Visit

Due to its moderate Mediterranean climate, Cascais is a popular tourist destination all year long. An overview of Cascais's climate and the ideal time to visit is provided below:

1. **Spring (March to May)**: Cascais experience warm temperatures and beautiful flowering sceneries during the spring. With sporadic rains, the average temperature ranges from 13°C (55°F) to 20°C (68°F). Outdoor recreation, sightseeing, and discovering the area's natural beauties are all best during this time of year.

2. **Summer (June to August):** Due to the warm, bright weather, summer is Cascais' busiest travel season. Between 18°C (64°F) to 28°C (82°F), on average, are the hottest months of July and August. This is a popular period for outdoor activities, and you may enjoy a

variety of water sports at the beaches. Due to great demand, it is advised to reserve lodging and activities in advance.

3. **Autumn (September to November):** Cascais experience pleasant temperatures and fewer tourists throughout the autumn months. Between 16°C (61°F) and 24°C (75°F), on average, are the temperatures.

If you prefer calmer settings and agreeable weather, now is a fantastic time to visit. The nearby locations, including Sintra, have autumn foliage, which enhances the natural beauty.

4. **Winter (December to February):** Cascais experiences warm winters, with average lows of 9°C (48°F) and highs of 16°C (61°F). Rainfall is often mild, even though it is the wettest time

of the year. Wintertime provides a tranquil atmosphere and cheaper hotel rates. It's a fantastic time to see historical places, take part in cultural events, and experience regional food.

Overall, personal preferences and interests determine the best time to visit Cascais. The best seasons for great weather, less crowds, and outdoor activities are spring and fall. Beach lovers and those looking for exciting festivals and events will love summer. With the benefit of cheaper rates and more comfortable temperatures, winter offers a tranquil experience.

It's important to keep in mind that Cascais regularly hosts events and festivals, such as the Festas do Mar in August, which will heighten the thrill of your trip.

Local Customs and Etiquette

To ensure a polite and delightful experience when visiting Cascais, it is necessary to become familiar with the regional customs and etiquette. To remember, have the following in mind:

1. Greetings and decorum

- The majority of Portuguese people are hospitable and pleasant. It is usual to extend a handshake and make eye contact when greeting.

- When speaking with natives, be sure to use courteous greetings like "Bom dia," "Boa tarde," and "Boa noite."

- Unless otherwise requested, refer to them by their titles, such as "Senhor" (Mr.) and "Senhora" (Mrs./Ms.), followed by their last name.

2. Fashion Code:

- Although Cascais is a laid-back beach town, it is still advisable to dress modestly, especially when visiting luxury shops or places of worship.

- Only the beach or pool areas are appropriate for wearing beachwear.

3. Punctuality:

- In Portugal, being on time is valued. It's a good idea to be on time for meetings, appointments, and tours.

4. Dining Manners:

- It is normal to say hello to the staff while entering and leaving a restaurant when dining out.

- Attend the host or hostess's cue to choose a seat.

- While dining, keep your hands on the table; putting them in your lap could be considered rude.

- Eat everything on your plate because leaving food on a dish might be viewed as waste.

- If a service charge is not included in the bill, it is usual to tip roughly 10% of the entire amount.

5. Language:

- It's welcome if you try to learn a few simple Portuguese expressions like "Obrigado/a" (Thank you) and "Por favour" (Please), even if many folks in Cascais understand English.

6. Honouring Culture and Traditions

- When visiting religious places, monuments, and museums, be respectful. Observe any instructions or rules given.

- If not allowed, refrain from touching or climbing on old buildings or relics.

7. The volume of Noise:

- To respect the quietness of the neighbourhood, keep noise levels down, especially at night and during the evening hours.

8. Environmental Awareness

- The city of Cascais is dedicated to ecotourism. By properly disposing of rubbish and utilising appropriate bins, you can contribute to keeping the beaches and natural areas clean.

Respecting the culture and traditions of Cascais by keeping in mind certain regional customs and etiquette can help you build goodwill with the populace and improve your trip as a whole.

PLANNING YOUR TRIP

Travel Essentials

To ensure a pleasant and happy journey, it's important to bring a few necessities when making travel plans to Cascais. The following is a list of things you might want to bring:

1. Travel papers:

- The passport must be current (check the expiration date and confirm that it fits the conditions for entrance).

- If a visa is needed (based on your nationality), obtain one.

- Your travel itinerary, reservations for lodging, and any relevant confirmations, in printed or digital form.

2. Banking and Finance:

- Enough cash in local currency (Euros) on hand to cover little costs or emergencies.

- For larger transactions and ATM withdrawals, use credit or debit cards.

- To prevent any problems with card usage, inform your bank or credit card provider of your vacation plans.

3. Travel Protection:

- A thorough travel insurance plan that includes coverage for medical emergencies, trip cancellation or interruption, and lost or delayed luggage.

4. Drugs and medical equipment:

- Medications on prescription, with a copy of the prescription.

- Basic medical items including bandages, painkillers, antihistamines, etc. are included in a personal first-aid kit.
- All essential immunizations or preventative drugs that your doctor may advise.

5. Communications and electronics:

- phone and charger for it.

- power adapter (if your country's plugs are a different type).

- For on-the-go gadget charging, a portable power bank.

- Use a camera or a smartphone to record special occasions.

- If necessary, a portable Wi-Fi device or SIM card for internet access.

6. Accessories and Clothes

- Appropriate footwear for walking around town and participating in outdoor activities.

- Choose season-appropriate attire that is light and breathable.

- For beach days, bring your swimsuit, sunglasses, and a sun hat.

- A lightweight sweater or jacket for chilly evenings.

- When travelling during the rainy season, bring rain gear (an umbrella or a raincoat).

7. Personal care and hygiene products

- Personal hygiene supplies, such as soap, toothpaste, and toothbrushes.

- High SPF sun protection.

- Anti-insect spray.

- convenient toiletries in travel sizes.

8. Electronic devices and travel adapters:

- To ensure compatibility with regional electrical outlets, use adapter plugs.

- For enjoyment, while travelling, bring along portable technology (such as tablets and e-readers).

Keep some food on hand for when you're travelling or exploring far-off places.

Keep in mind to pack for the particular season and activities you intend to partake in while in Cascais. It's a good idea to check the weather forecast closer to your departure date to see if your packing list needs to be modified.

Visa and Entry Requirements

It's critical to understand the admission criteria for Cascais, Portugal, depending on your nationality. The Portuguese embassy or consulate in your nation should always be consulted for the most recent and correct information despite the broad information provided here.

1. Area Schengen:

- Portugal is a part of the Schengen Area, which enables some nationalities to travel without a visa between its member states.

- Use a valid national ID card or passport to enter Portugal if you are a citizen of a Schengen Area country.

2. Visa-free travel:

- The majority of European Union (EU) nations, as well as the United States, Canada, Australia, New Zealand, and Japan, do not require a visa for entry into Portugal for leisure or business.

- In general, a visa-free stay is only allowed for 90 days out of every 180 days.

3. Entry Requires a Visa:

- Before visiting Portugal, citizens of various nations, including numerous African and Asian nations, Russia, China, and India, must get a visa.

- For comprehensive information on the requirements and application process for Portuguese visas, get in touch with the Portuguese embassy or consulate in your nation.

4. The Schengen Visa

- If you want to travel to several Schengen nations and are not qualified for visa-free entry, you may need to apply for a Schengen visa.

- You can travel to the Schengen Area for up to 90 days at a time (for tourism, business, or other authorised purposes) with a Schengen visa.

- Visit the Portuguese embassy or consulate in your nation to request a Schengen visa.

5. Documents needed to apply for a visa:

- The passport must be valid for at least six months beyond the desired stay.

- Filled out the visa application.

- A copy of the travel itinerary, including the flight and hotel reservations.

- A copy of your travel insurance policy showing that it covers medical emergencies and repatriation.

- Proof that you have the resources to sustain your stay in Portugal.

- Additional records as necessary, such as bank statements, employment letters, or invitation letters.

Keep in mind that as processing timelines can vary, you should apply for your visa well in advance of the dates you intend to travel. It is advised to gather all relevant paperwork, complete the application correctly, and deliver any additional supporting documents requested by the embassy or consulate.

It's crucial to remember that visa and entry criteria can change, so it's always advisable to confirm the most recent requirements with the relevant authorities or seek advice from a travel agency or immigration lawyer to guarantee a simple and trouble-free admission into Cascais and Portugal.

Accommodation Options

A variety of lodging choices are available in Cascais to accommodate different spending limits and tastes. There are many options in and around the town, whether you're seeking high-end hotels, stylish guesthouses, or affordable lodging. Here are a few popular forms of lodging in Cascais:

1. Resorts and Hotels:

- **Luxury Hotels:** There are several opulent hotels and resorts in Cascais that provide first-rate amenities, spa services, exquisite cuisine, and breathtaking ocean views.

- **Boutique Hotels**: In the town centre are charming boutique hotels that offer individualised service and distinctive design features.

- **Mid-Range Hotels**: Many mid-range hotels offer decent lodging at reasonable rates, frequently in convenient locations close to the town centre or the beach.

2. Bed and breakfasts and guesthouses:

- Guesthouses and bed and breakfast companies offer a warm and welcoming ambiance, frequently run by welcoming hosts who provide attentive service and local knowledge.

- Many guest houses provide a home-like feel and are situated close to the beach or within walking distance of the town centre.

3. Apartments and vacation rentals:

- In Cascais, renting a holiday house or apartment is a common choice. For families or longer visits, this enables a more independent stay with greater room and facilities like a kitchen.

- You can pick from a variety of flats, villas, or beachfront properties on several internet portals that provide a wide selection of Cascais vacation rental possibilities.

4. Hostels:

- Hostels offer inexpensive dormitory-style lodging with shared amenities including community kitchens and common areas for tourists on a tight budget or looking for a social environment.

- More privacy alternatives are available at several Cascais hostels that also provide private rooms.

5. Parks for tent camping and RVs:

- Camping and RV sites are available in and near Cascais for outdoor enthusiasts. This enables a close relationship with nature and frequently includes amenities like showers, laundries, and entertainment areas.

Consider things like location, amenities, closeness to activities, and your budget while selecting lodging in Cascais. To secure the greatest alternatives and prices, it is important to make reservations in advance, especially during the summer months when tourism is at its peak.

Finding appropriate lodging that satisfies your particular needs can be facilitated by online travel services, hotel websites, and travel companies.

To ensure a relaxing and convenient stay in Cascais, consider the particular needs and preferences of your vacation, such as access to the beach, closeness to public transit, or access to particular activities.

Transportation in and around Cascais

Numerous modes of transportation are available in Cascais for moving around the city and discovering the surroundings. The primary forms of transportation are as follows:

1. Train:

- Between Cascais and Lisbon, the railway is a practical and well-liked mode of transportation. The two cities are connected by the Cascais Line, which runs frequently all day.

- The train ride from Lisbon to Cascais lasts between 30 and 40 minutes, stopping at several stations along the way.

- Air-conditioned and comfortable, trains provide beautiful views of the shoreline.

2. Bus:

- There is a vast local bus network in Cascais that serves the city and its environs. The local transportation provider, Scotturb, runs buses.

- Buses connect several Cascais areas with surrounding tourist destinations including Guincho Beach and the town of Sintra.

- Bus routes and schedules are available through the Cascais Tourism Office or online.

3. Taxi:

- In Cascais, taxis are easily accessible and may be obtained at marked taxi stands or by hailing one on the street.

- Taxis have a metered fare system, so it's best to make sure the metre is turned on before setting out on your trip.

- Taxis might be a practical choice for quick travels or while carrying bags.

4. Auto rental

- For flexibility and convenience while touring Cascais and its surroundings, rent a car.

- In Cascais, there are locations for several vehicle rental companies, including near the train station and in the town centre.

- It's crucial to become familiar with the area's traffic laws, parking restrictions, and any tolls that might be necessary.

5. Bicycles:

- With designated bike lanes and bike-sharing schemes, Cascais is a bike-friendly community.

- An excellent way to get around town at your leisure, take beautiful coastline rides, or get to local beaches is by renting a bicycle.

6. Walking:

- The small village of Cascais is conveniently walkable.

- You can easily walk to the town centre, beaches, and several attractions, soaking up the quaint ambiance and finding hidden jewels.

7. Electric bicycles and scooters:

- In Cascais, electric scooters and bikes can be rented for a fun and eco-friendly way to go around the city and its surroundings.

It's important to note that Cascais is well connected to other adjacent cities like Estoril and Sintra, making day trips using the different modes of transportation simple to arrange.

When selecting the best means of transportation in and around Cascais, keep in mind to take your particular requirements, your spending limit, and the distance to your intended locations into account.

Safety Tips and Emergency Information

It's critical to put your safety first when visiting Cascais and to be ready for unexpected emergencies. Keep in mind the following safety advice and emergency contact information:

1. Safety precautions in general:

- Keep an eye out for pickpockets and other small-time criminals when in busy places or popular tourist destinations. Use a money belt or a secret pouch to keep your valuables safe.

- Avoid going alone at night or in dimly lit, lonely regions.

- Avoid taking rides from unmarked or unofficial vehicles and instead use licensed taxis or reliable transportation services.

- Respect local customs and laws as well as the rules and regulations of the area.

2. Numerals for emergencies

- For quick assistance in an emergency, dial 112 for emergency services (police, ambulance, and fire).

- Police Station in Cascais (PSP): +351 214 823 630

- Hospital de Cascais: +351 214 815 100

3. Facilities for health and medicine:

- If required, Cascais offers hospitals and medical facilities that can offer the required medical care.

- It is important to have travel insurance that includes emergency medical evacuation and coverage for medical costs.

- Make sure you have enough of any prescription or medication you may need for the duration of your stay by bringing it with you.

4. Coastal Safety:

- It's crucial to abide by safety precautions when visiting the beaches in Cascais. Pay attention to any caution flags or signs that indicate rough seas, and follow any lifeguards' instructions.

- Swim only in locations that have been marked, and watch out for strong currents.

- Watch out for young swimmers and unskilled swimmers.

- Regularly use sunscreen to shield your skin from the sun's rays.

5. Natural Risks:

- Although Cascais is generally a safe place to visit, it is important to be aware of any potential natural risks, like extreme weather or wildfires.

- Examine the local weather forecast and pay attention to any cautions or warnings issued by the authorities.

- In case an evacuation or other safety precautions are advised, heed the local authorities' recommendations.

6. Travel Warning:

- Keep abreast of any travel warnings or alerts sent out by the embassy or consulate of your country in Portugal.

- Inform your embassy or consulate of your travel arrangements so that they can help you if necessary.

7. Language and Communication

- Although English is widely spoken in tourist regions, learning a few fundamental Portuguese words will help you converse with locals.

- To stay connected in case of crises, have a functional mobile phone with a local SIM card or an international roaming plan.

Keep in mind that taking safety precautions can greatly improve your vacation experience. To have a secure and pleasurable trip to Cascais, be informed, cautious, and trust your senses.

EXPLORING CASCAIS

Cascais City Center

The bustling centre of the town, Cascais City Center, offers a blend of contemporary conveniences and historical charm. Here is a general description of what to expect while touring Cascais City Center:

1. 5th of October Square (Praça 5 de Outubro):

- Cascais' centre square is renowned for its lovely palm trees and fountain in the middle.

- A popular gathering spot for locals and tourists that is flanked by cafes, eateries, and stores.

- Frequently hosts cultural events, street fairs, and live musical performances.

2. Straight Street, or Rua Direita:

- The main pedestrian street contains stores, boutiques, and cafes in the heart of the city.

- Ideal for taking a stroll, looking for gifts, or having a meal or coffee.

3. Marina in Cascais:

- The marina, which lies in the heart of the city, is a centre of activity for yachts and boats.

- Provides a beautiful waterfront location that is studded with restaurants, bars, and cafes.

- Excellent location for enjoying a sunset stroll, observing the boats, or people-watching.

4. Condes de Castro Guimarães Museum

- A former home turned museum close to the city's heart.
- Displays a substantial collection of rare books, ceramics, furniture, and art.

- Gives a picture of the former aristocratic lifestyle.

5. Citadel of Cascais (Cidadela de Cascais):

- A former stronghold turned cultural hub close to the city's core.

- Contains artisan stores, exhibition halls, and art galleries.

- Frequently holds cultural events, plays, and art exhibitions.

6. Cultural Center of Cascais:

- A cutting-edge cultural centre that presents a range of creative and cultural events.

- includes film screenings, theatre productions, concerts, and art exhibits.

- Near the train station and in the heart of the city.

7. Market in Cascais:

- The market, also known as Mercado da Vila, is a lively location for local goods, gourmet foods, and fresh vegetables.

- Provides a variety of stalls where you may buy fruits, vegetables, cheeses, fish, pastries, and other foods.

- A fantastic location to experience the regional cuisine and take in the lively environment.

8. Town Hall of Cascais:

- A stunning structure situated in the heart of the city, close to 5th of October Square.

- Features historical significance and gorgeous architecture.

- Offers escorted tours so that visitors can explore the interior and discover the town's history.

9. Shops at Cascais Villa:

- In the heart of the city, near the train station, is a contemporary shopping area.

- Has a grocery, as well as a variety of stores, boutiques, and restaurants.

- Offers a handy choice for dining, shopping, or seeing a movie.

A lively and inviting ambiance is created by the combination of historical sites, cultural hubs, retail stores, and food options in Cascais City Center.

It's a must-see location if you want to experience the local culture firsthand and take in the bustling atmosphere of this coastal town.

Praia do Guincho

The famous beach Praia do Guincho lies about 8 kilometres (5 miles) northwest of Cascais. For surfers, windsurfers, and kitesurfers, it is a well-liked location due to its stunning natural scenery and powerful waves. What you should know about Praia do Guincho is as follows:

1. Natural Beauty

- Within the Sintra-Cascais Natural Park, Praia do Guincho offers breathtaking natural settings.

- The beach is surrounded by lovely dunes, and the untamed Serra de Sintra mountains form a striking backdrop.

- The immaculate sandy beach reaches a length of 800 metres (2,600 feet), and the Atlantic Ocean's waves batter it.

2. Aquatic Sports

- Praia do Guincho is a popular destination for lovers of water sports due to its exceptional wind and wave conditions.

- Due to the high winds and reliable waves, the beach is especially well-liked for kitesurfing, windsurfing, and surfing.

- Both novice and expert surfers hoping to catch some waves can find nearby surf schools and rental businesses.

3. Prevailing winds

- Guincho is renowned for having strong, reliable winds that normally come from the northwest and are perfect for wind-based sports.

- The tough conditions are great for windsurfers and kitesurfers, who can also benefit from the beach's fame as a premier windsurfing location.

4. Coastal amenities:

- Praia do Guincho provides a variety of comforts for visitors, including lifeguards on duty throughout the summer for enhanced security.

- Beachgoers can use the public restrooms, showers, and changing rooms.

- Visitors can unwind and enjoy the sun by renting sunbeds and umbrellas at the beach.

5. Natural Beauty and Coastal Trails:

- If you want to explore the beautiful coastline trails in the Sintra-Cascais Natural Park, Praia do Guincho is a great place to start.

- You can go riding and hiking on the paths, where you can take in the stunning views of the ocean and the untamed coastline.

6. Cafes and restaurants:

- There are several eateries and cafés at the beach and nearby that provide a variety of foods, including seafood and Portuguese delicacies.

- It's a wonderful chance to savour delectable seafood dishes while taking in the ocean vistas.

Praia do Guincho is a must-visit location for beach lovers and outdoor enthusiasts due to its breathtaking natural setting, exhilarating water sports options, and proximity to the Sintra-Cascais Natural Park.

Praia do Guincho offers an exceptional experience, regardless of whether you're an experienced surfer or just looking for a gorgeous beach to unwind and take in the surroundings.

Boca do Inferno

The captivating natural wonder known as Boca do Inferno, or "Hell's Mouth," is close to the town of Cascais. What you should know about Boca do Inferno is as follows:

1. Geographical setting

- Along Cascais' rocky shoreline, there is a distinctive cliff structure called Boca do Inferno.

- It was created by the Atlantic Ocean's constant battering of the limestone cliffs, which progressively eroded the rocks and left a gaping breach.

2. Dramatic Elements:

- The enormous, gaping pit that emerges in the cliffs, resembling a monstrous mouth, is Boca do Inferno's most notable feature.

- Waves flood into the cavern during times of high tide and stormy seas, creating a tremendous roar and a stunning exhibition of nature's power.

2. Beautiful views

- Views of the surrounding coastline and the vastness of the Atlantic Ocean are breathtaking from Boca do Inferno.

- The cliffs provide lookout platforms and walkways that let tourists take in the breathtaking panorama.

3. Opportunities for Photography:

- Boca do Inferno is a well-liked location for photographers who want to capture the unadulterated beauty of the surrounding terrain because of the towering rock formations and pounding waves.

- A compelling subject for photography is the sea's vibrant colours in contrast to the rocky rocks.

4. Facilities and Access:

- Boca do Inferno, which lies about 2 kilometres (1.2 miles) west of the centre of Cascais, is conveniently reachable on foot.

- It is an outdoor natural attraction, thus there is no admittance price or set closing time.

- Visitors can enjoy the view safely thanks to the area's paths and security walls.

5. Nearby landmarks

- Boca do Inferno is an easy stop on a coastal excursion because it is adjacent to other well-liked destinations like Praia do Guincho and the Cascais Marina.

- A trip to Boca do Inferno can be combined with a leisurely bike ride or stroll along the seaside route.

A trip to Boca do Inferno offers the chance to experience the unbridled power of nature and take in the breathtaking splendour of the Cascais coastline.

Boca do Inferno is an outstanding natural beauty, whether you're taking pictures, taking in the scenery, or just watching the waves crash.

Cabo da Roca

Near Cascais, on the westernmost tip of continental Europe, is the breathtaking headland known as Cabo da Roca. What you should know about Cabo da Roca is as follows:

1. Geographic Importance

- Because Cabo da Roca is the westernmost point of continental Europe, it attracts a lot of travellers who want to see this important landmark.

- The headland sits above soaring cliffs that plunge sharply into the Atlantic Ocean, offering stunning panoramic vistas.

2. Authentic Beauty

- One of Cabo da Roca's biggest draws is the rocky and spectacular coastal landscape. The cliffside setting provides breathtaking views of the ocean, complete with crashing waves and windswept vistas.

- Awe and admiration for nature are sparked by the unspoiled beauty of the surroundings and the size of the ocean.

3. Lighthouse:

- A beautiful lighthouse that acts as a landmark and a navigational aid may be found near Cabo da Roca.

- In contrast to the cliffs and ocean, the lighthouse creates a strong focus point that makes for a wonderful photo opportunity.

4. Information Desk for Visitors:

- There is a visitor centre in Cabo da Roca where you can find out more about the region's geology, history, and culture.

- Maps, brochures, and details about neighbouring activities and attractions are available at the centre.

5. Hiking routes

- Natural trails encircle Cabo da Roca, enabling guests to stroll throughout the area.

- Beautiful vistas and the possibility to learn more about the area's biodiversity and natural beauty may be found on the coastal hiking routes.

6. Merchandise store and café:

- At Cabo da Roca, you may buy keepsakes and have refreshments while admiring the picturesque surroundings in the souvenir shop and café.

7. Sunset Views

- When the sun sets, Cabo da Roca is especially well-liked because the cliffs and ocean are bathed in warm, golden tones.

- From this westernmost point of Europe, it is a wonderful experience to watch the sunset.

8. Accessibility:

- From Cascais or Sintra, one can travel to Cabo da Roca via automobile or public transit.

- Additionally, it is a stop on certain sightseeing trips that take in the region's prime attractions.
- The headland is exposed to Atlantic winds, so prepare for windy weather by dressing appropriately.

By going to Cabo da Roca, you can experience what it's like to be on the very edge of Europe.

Cabo da Roca is a must-visit location that displays the unadulterated force and beauty of the Atlantic coastline, regardless of your interest in its geographic significance, natural beauty, or sense of adventure.

Parque Marechal Carmona

The beautiful park Parque Marechal Carmona, sometimes referred to as Parque da Gandarinha, is situated in the centre of Cascais. It provides a serene haven of vegetation and a range of recreational pursuits. What to expect when visiting Parque Marechal Carmona is as follows:

1. Green Spaces and Lush Gardens:

- The park has well-kept gardens with an assortment of different kinds of plants, trees, and flowers.

- Enjoy the tranquil atmosphere that the park's natural beauty creates as you stroll along the winding walkways.

2. The playground for kids

- Children can enjoy a variety of play structures, swings, and slides in the playground section of Parque Marechal Carmona.

- Families may unwind there while the kids play and burn off some energy.

3. Areas for Picnics

- For a leisurely outdoor lunch or snack, the park has dedicated picnic spaces with benches and tables.

- Bring your meal or buy some regional specialties from stores close by to enjoy this peaceful environment.

4. Wildlife and a lake:

- A little lake at Parque Marechal Carmona is where you can see ducks and other wildlife.

- The lake enhances the beauty and tranquillity of the park.

5. Festivals and Events:

- Throughout the year, the park holds several festivals, concerts, and cultural events.

- If any noteworthy events are happening while you are there, check the local events calendar.

6. Municipal Library of Cascais:

- The Cascais Municipal Library, a contemporary building with a large selection of books, magazines, and multimedia services, is also located in Parque Marechal Carmona.

- Browse the collection, unwind in the reading spaces, or take part in literary events are all options for visitors.

7. Art installations and sculptures:

- Numerous sculptures and artworks can be found around the park as you stroll about and enjoy the surroundings.

- These creative touches improve the park's aesthetic appeal and present interesting photo possibilities.

8. Sporting Venues:

- For individuals looking for physical activity, Parque Marechal Carmona offers sporting amenities like tennis courts and a skate park.

9. The location is accessible.

- The park is conveniently situated in the heart of Cascais, close to the town's commercial district and public transportation hub.

- Due to the park's free admission, both locals and visitors frequent it.

In the centre of Cascais, Parque Marechal Carmona offers a tranquil hideaway where guests may unwind, commune with nature, and partake in a variety of recreational pursuits. This park provides a pleasant respite from the busy city centre, whether you're looking for a quiet stroll, a family adventure, or a spot to have a picnic.

Cascais Marina

A thriving waterfront neighbourhood in Cascais, Cascais Marina offers a mix of food options, leisure pursuits, and maritime elegance. What to anticipate when visiting Cascais Marina is as follows:

Maritime Ambience:

- The Cascais Marina is a hive of activity for people interested in boats and maritime pursuits.

- Yachts, sailboats, and fishing boats line the marina, giving it a stunning scene and a lively maritime ambiance.

Coastal Promenade:

- A beautiful area for a stroll may be found along the marina's well-kept promenade.

- Enjoy the picturesque views of the yachts, the marina's sparkling waters, and the nearby coastline.

Cafes and restaurants:

- There are many beachfront restaurants and cafés in Cascais Marina.

- Fresh seafood, traditional Portuguese fare, cosmopolitan cuisine, and attractive seaside cafes are just a few of the gastronomic options available.

Terraces and outdoor seating areas:

- You may enjoy your meal or beverage with a view of the marina and the ocean at many of the cafes and restaurants in Cascais Marina thanks to their outdoor seating areas and terraces.

Activities on the water and boat excursions:

- The Cascais Marina offers a variety of boat tours and watersports.

- For those looking for a more opulent experience on the water, there are boat tours around the coast, sailing excursions, fishing charters, and even yacht rentals.

Water sports and sailing schools:

- For individuals who want to take up sailing or other water sports, Cascais Marina is a great location.

- Lessons, equipment rentals, and guided activities are available at the marina's sailing schools and water sports facilities.

Retail establishments:

- The marina area has a variety of boutique boutiques and establishments with nautical themes.

- Discover these businesses whether you're looking for trinkets, clothes, accessories, or boating supplies.

Festivals and Events:

- Events, regattas, and festivals centred around boating and marine pursuits are frequently held at Cascais Marina.

- If any noteworthy events are happening while you are there, check the local events calendar.

Sunset Views

- The Cascais Marina is a great location to watch a passionate sunset.

- Find a comfortable area on a restaurant terrace, the waterfront promenade, or on a boat tour to take in the sun's magnificent colours.

A mix of food, shopping, water sports, and a lively environment can be found in the lively and attractive waterfront neighbourhood known as Cascais Marina. A trip to Cascais Marina is likely to be a joy, whether you're a boating enthusiast, a foodie, or you're just looking to take in the seaside atmosphere.

BEACHES AND WATER ACTIVITIES

Top Beaches in Cascais

The coastline of Cascais is blessed with many stunning beaches. These Cascais beaches are among the best and should be visited:

Guincho Beach:

- Praia do Guincho, which is about 8 kilometres (5 miles) northwest of Cascais, is renowned for its breathtaking natural beauty and great wind and surf conditions.

- Due to its high winds and reliable waves, it is a preferred location for surfers, windsurfers, and kitesurfers.

- A lovely environment is provided by the wide sandy beach, which is bordered by dunes and the Sintra-Cascais Natural Park.

Rainha Beach:

- Small and endearing Praia da Rainha, often known as "Queen's Beach," is tucked away in a lovely cove in the middle of Cascais.

- It is renowned for its serene ambiance, glistening waves, and surrounding cliffs.

- The beach offers a nice place to unwind and enjoy the sun and is conveniently located.

The Beach of Conception:

- One of the principal beaches in Cascais, Praia da Conceiço is situated close to the town's centre.

- It has a long stretch of fine, golden sand, crystal-clear water, and a range of beachside facilities.

- Visitors may easily access the beach thanks to the promenade's restaurants, cafés, and stores.

Beach at Duquesa:

- Another well-liked beach near Cascais's town is Praia da Duquesa.

- With a protected bay and tranquil surf, it provides a serene and welcoming atmosphere for families.

- The beach is renowned for providing stunning views of Cascais Bay and the quaint Duquesa Docks.

Tamariz Beach:

- Praia do Tamariz is a bustling and well-liked beach that is close to Cascais in the surrounding Estoril city.

- It has a broad sandy beach, calm waves, and a promenade dotted with beachside cafes, bars, and eateries.

- The beach provides several amenities, such as showers, lifeguard services, and the ability to rent sun loungers and umbrellas.

The beach at Moitas:

- Small and isolated Praia das Moitas beach is tucked between rocky cliffs and provides a more serene and private atmosphere.

- It's a wonderful location for tanning while taking in the natural beauty of the shoreline.

- It should be noted that Praia das Moitas may only be reached by descending a staircase, adding to its remoteness.

These are only a few of Cascais' best beaches, each of which has its distinct appeal and qualities. Cascais features beaches to fit your preferences, whether you're looking for thrilling water activities, kid-friendly settings, or beautiful coastal scenery.

Surfing, Windsurfing and Kitesurfing

Due to its ideal wind and wave conditions, Cascais is an excellent location for kitesurfing, windsurfing, and surfing. What you need to know about these water activities in Cascais is as follows:

Surfing:

1. **Praia do Guincho**: Known as one of the top surfing locations in the region, Praia do Guincho is perfect for seasoned surfers due to its reliable waves and strong winds.

- Surfers of various skill levels frequent Carcavelos Beach, which is close to Cascais. It offers consistent surfing and a variety of surf schools where novices can enrol in instruction.

Windsurfing:

1. **Praia do Guincho:** Praia do Guincho is a sanctuary for windsurfers thanks to its strong and reliable winds. It is appropriate for experienced riders because of the strong waves and windy gusts.

- **Carcavelos Beach**: Carcavelos Beach is popular with windsurfers as well, who love the steady breezes and room to manoeuvre.

Kitesurfing:

- **Lagoa de Albufeira:** Just outside of Cascais, Lagoa de Albufeira is a well-liked place for kiteboarding. It is appropriate for both novice and expert riders due to its shallow waters and consistent breezes.

- **Guincho Beach:** Known for such strong winds, Guincho Beach is an exhilarating location for kitesurfing. Kitesurfers of all skill levels are drawn to the area by its expansive sandy beach and reliable wind conditions.

It's important to keep in mind that wind and wave conditions might change with the season and weather patterns. In Cascais, the winds are generally more steady in the spring and fall, making those seasons the ideal times for kitesurfing, windsurfing, and surfing.

There are many surf schools and water sports facilities in Cascais that offer lessons, equipment rentals, and guided excursions whether you're new to these sports or want to hone your abilities. They can give you the tools you need and qualified instruction to get going or improve your skills.

Always put safety first by following local laws, using the proper safety gear, and being considerate of other beachgoers and water users.

Sailing and Boating

Sailing and boating enthusiasts should visit Cascais since it offers a variety of opportunities for exploring the coastline and taking in the Atlantic waters. What you need to know about sailing and boating in Cascais is as follows:

Yacht rentals and charters:

- A popular location for yacht rentals and charters, Cascais Marina offers the chance to sail around the breathtaking coastline.

- Several businesses hire out a variety of sailboats, motorboats, and luxury yachts, either with or without a skipper.

- By renting a boat, you may create your itinerary and take your time discovering the neighbouring coves, beaches, and sights.

Sailing Instruction and Schools:

- Cascais has several sailing schools and training facilities if you're interested in learning to sail or sharpening your sailing abilities.

- Depending on your ability level, knowledgeable instructors can coach you in advanced techniques or walk you through the fundamentals.

- Individual, couple, or group sailing courses are available, providing an enjoyable and instructive experience.

Events for sailing and regattas:

- Cascais has a long history of hosting sailing competitions and regattas.

- If you enjoy sailing, you might be able to watch or take part in one of the regional or international tournaments that are taking place in Cascais.

- To see whether any regattas or sailing events coincide with your visit, check the local events calendar.

Boat Tours and Coastal Cruises:

- From Cascais, several businesses offer boat trips and coastal cruises that let you take a leisurely ride down the coast.

- These guided tours give panoramic views of the beautiful coastline as well as information about the history, geology, and marine life of the area.

- Depending on your preferences, boat cruises might range from brief outings to half-day or full-day excursions.

Fishing excursions:

- If you enjoy fishing, Cascais provides fishing excursions that will make your trip to the water enjoyable.

- Whether you're interested in deep-sea fishing or fishing closer to the shore, knowledgeable local captains can take you to the greatest fishing locations.

- Fishing charters often offer all the gear and instruction required for a pleasurable fishing trip.

It's vital to remember that weather and sea conditions might affect boating and sailing operations. Check the weather forecast before leaving, abide by safety precautions, and make sure you have the necessary safety gear on board.

To accommodate a variety of tastes and experiences, Cascais offers a variety of activities, including sailing, boat rentals, and boat tours. It's a wonderful way to savour the splendour of the Atlantic Ocean, explore the coastline, and find undiscovered coves.

Diving and Snorkelling

Dive and snorkelling chances are superb in Cascais, allowing you to explore the underwater world and learn about the local marine fauna. What you should know about snorkelling and scuba diving in Cascais is as follows:

Diving:

1. **Dive Sites:** The coastline of Cascais is home to many dive sites, each of which offers distinctive marine life, underwater scenery, and diving opportunities.

2. **Pedra do Sal:** A well-liked dive location close to Cascais, Pedra do Sal is renowned for its rocky formations and varied marine habitat. It provides chances to see different kinds of fish, vibrant sponges, and underwater caverns.

3. Mar do Inferno: Also known as the "Sea of Hell," Mar do Inferno is a well-known dive location known for its magnificent rock formations and underwater tunnels. For more experienced divers, it offers a fun diving experience.

4. **Dive facilities:** Cascais has dive facilities that provide guided diving excursions, equipment rentals, and diving courses for divers of all abilities, from novices to experts. To guarantee a safe and fun diving experience, these centres can offer essential equipment, safety courses, and local knowledge.

5. **Marine life:** A wide variety of marine species can be found in the waters near Cascais. You might come across species while diving, including sea bream, wrasse, octopus, moray eels, and vibrant nudibranchs. During the proper season, keep an eye out for the

uncommon sightings of sunfish (Mola mola), or perhaps the occasional meeting with dolphins.

Snorkelling:

1. Snorkelling Locations: Cascais has some great locations for snorkelling, particularly around its rocky coves and crystal-clear seas.

2. Apart from being well-known for its surfing and windsurfing, Praia do Guincho also offers fantastic snorkelling chances. Small fish, crabs, and sea anemones can be found by exploring the shallow areas near the coast.

3. **Praia da Ribeira**: This snorkelling destination, which is close to the Cascais Marina, has calm seas and intriguing undersea structures.

4. **Equipment**: Dive shops and beachside stores in Cascais lend out snorkelling gear, like masks, snorkels, and fins. If you'd rather, you can bring your equipment.

Safety considerations When diving or snorkelling, safety must always come first:

- Always dive or snorkel with a buddy, and observe all safety precautions.

- Be mindful of your surroundings, particularly any currents and potential dangers underwater.

- Don't touch or damage the underwater environment to show respect for marine life and the delicate ecosystem.

- It is advised to examine local weather conditions, tides, and any potential limits or rules issued by local authorities or dive shops before diving or snorkelling.

In Cascais, diving and snorkelling offer the chance to discover the region's underwater treasures and take in its abundant marine variety. Everyone interested in diving, whether they are novices or experts, or simply love snorkelling, will find something to enjoy at Cascais.

Beach Safety and Tips

Prioritising safety is essential when visiting the beaches in Cascais to have a relaxing and worry-free experience. Following are some advice and rules for beach safety:

1. **Swim in approved places**: Refrain from swimming anywhere other than in approved swimming places when lifeguards are present. Flags or markers

are frequently used to designate these places. Lifeguards are prepared to respond to crises and offer help if required.

2. Watch for Warning Flags: Keep an eye out for flags or banners that warn of hazardous marine conditions. Important information such as heavy surf, strong currents, or hazardous circumstances can be conveyed by these flags. It's critical to pay attention to these cautions and steer clear of risky swimming situations.

3. **Respect the Ocean**: Because the ocean is unpredictable, it is important to recognize its strength and its perils. Rip currents, which are powerful underwater currents that can drag swimmers away from the shore, should be avoided. Swim parallel to the coast until you are free of the current's pull if

you find yourself caught in one, then swim back to shore.

4. Children Must Be Supervised: If you're taking kids to the beach, make sure you keep a tight check on them at all times. To protect their safety while in or around the water, kids should constantly be watched. Inform children of water safety precautions and the value of remaining near the shore.

5. **Sun Protection:** Use sunscreen with a high SPF, and wear a helmet, sunglasses, and UV-protective clothes to shield yourself from the sun's damaging rays. Regularly reapply sunscreen, especially after swimming or perspiring.

6. **Keep Hydrated:** It's critical to keep hydrated while at the beach. To avoid

dehydration, bring lots of water and consume it frequently.

7. **Consider the Environment**: By properly disposing of waste in designated bins, you can help keep the beaches clean and save the environment. Respect the environment and refrain from destroying or removing any flora or marine life.

8. Prepare for your beach trip by packing necessary goods including towels, shade (such as umbrellas or sunshades), snacks, and water. A first aid kit, any necessary prescriptions, and any specific gear for aquatic sports should also be packed.

9. **Follow Local Regulations:** Become familiar with any local beach regulations, such as those governing swimming, boating, or particular water

sports. To protect your safety and the safety of others, abide by these rules.

Prepare for emergencies by becoming familiar with the locations of the nearest emergency services and lifeguard stations. Save emergency phone numbers in your phone and be aware of how to send an emergency message to your location.

You may enjoy your time at the beaches in Cascais while protecting your safety and the safety of others by adhering to these beach safety recommendations.

For a relaxing and enjoyable beach experience, keep in mind to exercise your best judgement, be aware of your surroundings, and appreciate the strength of the ocean.

CULTURAL EXPERIENCES

Museu Condes de Castro Guimarães

A cultural treasure in Cascais é o Museu Condes de Castro Guimarães, também referido como o Condes de Castro Guimarães Museum.

The museum, which is housed in a magnificent estate, provides a fascinating look into the history, culture, and traditions of the area. What to expect when visiting the Museu Condes de Castro Guimarães is as follows:

Old-fashioned home:

- The splendid palace that now serves as the museum was first constructed in the early 20th century as a private residence for the Portuguese Count of Castro Guimares.

- Turrets, balconies, and elaborate decorations define the mansion's architecture, which is a fusion of Gothic, Renaissance, and Manueline styles.

Artwork collection

- The museum displays a wide range of artistic works from many historical and stylistic eras.

- You may enjoy artwork such as paintings, sculptures, furniture, ceramics, and decorative arts that provide insights into Cascais and Portugal's cultural past.

Interiors from the past

- Discover the mansion's exquisitely restored interiors, which feature elegant chambers with detailed woodwork, tile panels, and antique furnishings.

- The mansion's sumptuous atmosphere offers a window into the previous aristocratic way of life.

Manuscripts and Rare Books:

- The library of the museum is home to an impressive collection of rare books, manuscripts, and papers that showcase the tastes of the Count of Castro Guimares.

- Book lovers and history buffs will value the chance to view these priceless literary artefacts.

Grounds and Gardens:

- Landscaped grounds and well-kept gardens encircle the museum.

- Take a stroll through the gardens, which are filled with lush vegetation, sculptures, and quiet areas where you can unwind and take in the pleasant ambiance.

Cultural gatherings and displays:

- Throughout the year, the Museu Condes de Castro Guimaraes offers several transient exhibitions, cultural gatherings, and educational activities.

- If there are any special exhibitions or events taking place during your visit, check the museum's calendar.

Ocean Views:

- Beautiful views of the Atlantic Ocean and the Cascais coastline may be seen from the museum's location.

- Enjoy the beautiful views for a moment and consider how the museum's history relates to its coastal location.

A fascinating experience can be had by visiting the Museu Condes de Castro Guimarães, which combines history, art, and architecture in a stunning home setting.

The museum in Cascais offers a singular and enriching experience, whether you're an art aficionado, a history buff, or just looking for a peaceful cultural vacation.

Casa das Histórias Paula Rego

The Paula Rego House of Stories, also known as Casa das Histórias Paula Rego, is an outstanding museum devoted to the life and works of the well-known Portuguese artist Paula Rego.

This museum, which is situated in Cascais, provides an enthralling voyage into the universe of one of Portugal's most renowned contemporary painters. What to expect when you travel to Casa das Histórias Paula Rego is as follows:

Construction and Design:

- The museum was created by renowned architect Eduardo Souto de Moura and is a work of art in and of itself.

- The building's distinctive style and vivid red hue stand out against the background scenery.

Artist Paula Rego:

- Paula Rego's artwork is on display in Casa das Histórias in a variety of media, including paintings, drawings, prints, and sculptures.

- Rego's work is renowned for its distinct style and frequent exploration of feminism, social justice, and narrative themes.

Temporary and Permanent Exhibitions:

- Paula Rego's artistic path can be fully experienced at the museum's permanent and temporary displays.

- The temporary exhibitions frequently focus on certain periods, topics, or partnerships, while the permanent collection presents a wide variety of her works.

Narratives and Storytelling

- The museum strives to bring the narratives that frequently underlie Paula Rego's artwork to life.

- The display areas of the museum are created to convey a sense of storytelling and to transport visitors on a visual tour through Rego's storylines.

Educational Workshops and Programs:

- For guests of all ages, Casa do Histórias provides educational programs, workshops, and activities that let them interact deeply with Paula Rego's artwork.

- These presentations help viewers comprehend Rego's work better by shedding light on her creative process, methods, and topics.

Shop and Café at the Museum:

- In the museum's gift shop, you may choose from a variety of Paula Rego-related books, catalogues, prints, and trinkets.

- Additionally, there is a café where you can unwind, eat a snack, or drink coffee while considering the art you have just seen.

Landscapes and Gardens:

- Gardens and outdoor areas that have been expertly manicured surround Casa das Histórias.

- The gardens offer a tranquil setting that gives visitors a chance to unwind and take in the natural beauty that served as the inspiration for Paula Rego's artwork.

You have a one-of-a-kind chance to immerse yourself in the mesmerising world of Paula Rego's work by going to Casa das Histórias Paula Rego.

This museum in Cascais offers a remarkable trip into the craftsmanship and narrative of one of Portugal's most renowned painters, whether you're a lover of her work, interested in modern art, or just seeking a thought-provoking cultural experience.

Cascais Cultural Center

The Centro Cultural de Cascais, popularly known as the Cascais Cultural Center, is a thriving cultural centre situated in the city of Cascais. Numerous artistic and cultural events, exhibitions, performances, and educational activities are held in this multipurpose facility. What to expect when you go to the Cascais Cultural Center is as follows:

Exhibitions:

- A changing schedule of exhibitions, including paintings, sculptures, photographs, and multimedia projects, are featured at the centre.

- The exhibitions frequently feature both domestic and foreign artists, offering a venue for creative expression and advancing cultural diversity.

Theatrical Arts:

- Theatre performances, dance performances, music concerts, and live performances are just a few of the performing arts events that are held in the Cascais Cultural Center.

- The centre's auditorium offers a contemporary and cosy atmosphere for these artistic events, giving the audience a unique experience.

Movie theatres and the cinema

- Films from various genres and cultures, including independent films, documentaries, and vintage films, are periodically shown at the centre.

- These showings provide a chance to experience thought-provoking and inspirational films in a social setting.

Seminars and educational pursuits:

- Workshops, lectures, and other educational events are organised by the Cascais Cultural Center to advance creative and cultural education.

- With these programs, people of all ages and interests can develop their creativity, pick up new skills, and participate in the arts.

Cultural Festivals and Events:

- The centre is a buzzing location for cultural celebrations of art, music, dance, and regional customs.

- These gatherings frequently include performances, exhibits, workshops, and interactive activities, which make the environment lively and interesting for guests.

Bookstore and café:

- Visitors to the Cascais Cultural Center can unwind, enjoy a drink, or eat a light meal in the café.

- The centre also houses a bookstore with a variety of books, journals, and publications from other cultures.

Construction Design:

- The Cascais Cultural Center's cutting-edge interior decor and modern architecture combine to create an aesthetically pleasing and warm environment.

- Architectural elements of the building frequently mesh well with the nearby urban environment.

An innovative and exciting setting for artistic expression, intercultural dialogue, and civic involvement is the Cascais Cultural Center. Visits to this cultural centre in Cascais are enlightening and exciting experiences that highlight the area's thriving artistic and cultural landscape, whether you're interested in visual arts, performing arts, or cultural activities.

Music and Festivals in Cascais

The city of Cascais has a thriving music culture and is well-known for holding numerous festivals and events all year long. The town offers a wide variety of musical events, from regional shows to worldwide acts. The following is a list of concerts and festivals in Cascais:

Jazz Club in Cascais:

- A well-known location for live jazz performances by regional and international performers is the Cascais Jazz Club.

- It provides a cosy atmosphere for jazz fans to enjoy the music and highlights the abilities of both seasoned and rising players.

Holidays in March:

- The annual Festas do Mar music festival takes place in August next to Cascais Bay.

- Throughout the festival, notable Portuguese and foreign musicians will play a series of concerts featuring pop, rock, fado, and traditional Portuguese music.

Cascais Rhythm:

- Funk, soul, and groove music are all honoured during the Cascais Groove music event.

- The event, which takes place in Cascais, brings together musicians from both domestic and foreign countries, resulting in a lively and groovy ambiance.

Jazz Cascais out:

- A summertime music festival called Out Jazz Cascais is held around the town in various locations.

- Jazz, soul, and funk concerts are performed outside during the festival, which offers music fans a laid-back and pleasurable setting.

Cascais's Cultural Center:

- Numerous musical events, such as classical concerts, chamber music recitals, and contemporary music events, are routinely held at the Cultural Center of Cascais.

- These events, which frequently include both local and foreign musicians, offer the chance to sample a variety of musical styles.

Music festival in Cascais:

- Rock, pop, folk, and electronic music are among the many musical genres that are featured during the yearly Cascais Music Festival.

- The festival draws music lovers from all over since it includes local and foreign bands and artists.

Performances on the street and buskers:

- You can run into buskers and street entertainers as you wander the streets of Cascais, playing music for onlookers.

- These spontaneous performances provide a distinctive musical experience while enhancing the town's lively vibe.

The city of Cascais hosts numerous musical events and festivals all year long that appeal to a range of preferences and musical styles. You can probably find a musical event that meets your tastes, whether you enjoy jazz, rock, classical music, or other genres. To stay informed about forthcoming musical performances and festivals in the region, keep an eye on local event calendars, contact the Cascais Tourism Office, or follow neighbourhood music venues.

Traditional Cuisine and Restaurants

The bustling food scene of Cascais is well-known and features both traditional Portuguese fare and flavours from around the world. An overview of local cuisine is provided below, along with a list of some top restaurants in Cascais:

Typical Portuguese Cuisine:

- Salted codfish is sautéed with onions, eggs, and thin potato fries in the meal known as "Bacalhau à Brás."

- A hearty soup prepared with kale, potatoes, and Portuguese chorizo is called caldo verde.

- Pasteis de Bacalhau: Codfish cakes that are deep-fried and have a crunchy outside and tender interior.

- Grilled chicken marinated in a fiery Piri-Piri chilli sauce is known as Frango Piri-Piri.

- A savoury seafood rice meal made with a variety of shellfish and fragrant herbs is called arroz de marisco.

Restaurants that are suggested in Cascais:

- Mar do Inferno is a restaurant with delicious seafood and breathtaking ocean views that is close to the Boca do Inferno cliffs.

- Furnas do Guincho is a restaurant with a focus on regional cuisine that serves seafood and traditional Portuguese dishes close to Praia do Guincho.

- Intimate dining establishment Taberna Clandestina serves a combination of modern and traditional Portuguese meals made with regional and seasonal ingredients.

- Restaurante Dom Dinis is a traditional Portuguese eatery with a focus on grilled meats and seafood that is located in Cascais's old district.

- **O Pescador**: This eatery, which is close to the Cascais Marina, serves a range of fresh fish meals in a quaint beach setting.

- A Casa da Guia: This complex offers a variety of dining options, including

Portuguese cuisine, sushi, and Mediterranean-inspired food. It is situated on a stunning cliffside site.

- Tasca da Linha is a well-liked neighbourhood restaurant that serves traditional Portuguese fare in a relaxed and welcoming setting.

These are but a few of Cascais's numerous outstanding eateries. Numerous dining establishments catering to all interests and price ranges may be found by exploring the area. When visiting Cascais, don't be afraid to sample traditional Portuguese cuisine and get a taste of the local fare.

NATURE AND OUTDOOR ADVENTURES

The abundant natural beauty of Cascais gives many chances for outdoor pursuits. Here are some of the best outdoor activities and natural attractions in and near Cascais:

Natural Park of Sintra-Cascais:

- From the sea to the mountains, the enormous Sintra-Cascais Natural Park offers a variety of scenery, including woods, cliffs, and pristine beaches.

- Discover secret waterfalls, hike the park's paths, visit Sintra's historic palaces, and take in the expansive vistas from high vantage points.

Natural Reserve at Guincho:

- Just northwest of Cascais, the Guincho Natural Reserve is renowned for its beautiful dunes, untamed vegetation, and gorgeous Guincho Beach.

- Explore the reserve on foot or by hiking, take in the coastal landscape, and experience the might of the Atlantic Ocean as it slams against the cliffs.

Trails for hiking and mountain biking:

- Mountain bikers and hikers can choose from a variety of trails in and around Cascais.

- Discover the Sintra-Cascais Natural Park's well-marked trails, which range from simple beach paths to strenuous mountain treks, to fully immerse yourself in the outdoors and take in the spectacular scenery.

Putting greens in Cascais

- With several top-notch golf courses nearby, Cascais is a golfer's heaven.

- Some of the prominent golf courses where you may play a round of golf while surrounded by breathtaking scenery are Quinta da Marinha Golf Course, Oitavos Dunes, and Estoril Golf Club.

Whale and Dolphin Watching:

- Enjoy the excitement of whale and dolphin watching at Cascais.

- Join a boat excursion or tour to see these magnificent marine animals in their natural habitat, making lifelong memories and connecting with the ocean.

You may fully enjoy Cascais' and its surroundings' natural beauty by participating in these outdoor activities. To satiate outdoor aficionados, Cascais provides a variety of experiences, whether you're looking for adventure, leisure, or a connection with nature. When you go on outdoor excursions in Cascais, keep in mind to respect the environment, abide by local laws, and put safety first.

DAY TRIPS FROM CASCAIS

Sintra: The Enchanted Forest

Sintra, often known as the "Enchanted Forest," is a mesmerising location renowned for its verdant vistas, ethereal mood, and luxuriant flora. Why Sintra is sometimes compared to an enchanted forest is as follows:

Thick Forests:

- Sintra is encircled by thick forests that give the area a wonderful and surreal feel.

- Towering trees, such as old oaks, tall pines, and alien species, are abundant in the woodlands, resulting in a diversified and rich ecology.

Romantic construction:

- Many beautiful palaces and castles that mix well with the surrounding landscape may be seen in Sintra.

- The fairytale-like surroundings of Pena Palace, Quinta da Regaleira, and Monserrate Palace are well known for their quirky architecture, elaborate detailing, and breathtaking vistas.

Gloomy atmosphere

- The magical mist that frequently envelops Sintra adds to the city's allure.

- The forested hills and ancient ruins are made even more alluring by the gloomy backdrop, which intensifies the dramatic scenery.

Natural Park of Sintra-Cascais:

- The Sintra-Cascais Natural Park, a protected area that has huge woodlands, cliffs, and picturesque pathways, is where Sintra is situated.

- The natural splendour of the park, which includes secret waterfalls, verdant valleys, and striking cliffs, adds to Sinatra's attractiveness as an enchanted woodland.

Folktales and Myths:

- Folktales and traditions about supernatural creatures, hidden wealth, and underground caverns abound in Sintra.

- These legends, along with the picturesque surroundings, contribute to the idea that Sintra is a magical forest.

Parks and Gardens:

- Beautiful gardens and parks may be found in Sintra, which add to the city's allure.

- The National Palace of Sintra, Quinta da Regaleira, and Monserrate Gardens are well known for their exotic plants, peaceful ambiance, and hidden surprises.

You can lose yourself in a realm of magic and unmatched natural beauty by travelling to Sintra. Discover the wooded hills, stroll through the enchanted gardens, and take in the architectural marvels that make Sintra such a magical place. Prepare yourself to be mesmerised by the magic and attraction of this remarkable "Enchanted Forest."

Lisbon: The Vibrant Capital

Lisbon, the energetic capital of Portugal, is a city that emanates vitality, has a rich history, and combines old-world charm with contemporary vibrancy in a singular way. Lisbon is frequently said to as the capital with a dynamic culture for the following reasons:

Colourful Communities:

- The attractive and vibrant neighbourhoods of Alfama, Bairro Alto, and Mouraria are among Lisbon's most well-known features.

- These neighbourhoods have a pleasant and lively ambiance because of their tiny alleys, tiled facades, and colourful homes.

French music:

- The traditional Portuguese musical style known as fado is ingrained in Lisbon's cultural landscape.

- There are a lot of fado houses and restaurants in Lisbon where you can hear this passionate and emotional music performed live, which creates a genuine and lively atmosphere.

Historical Sites:

- Lisbon is home to numerous historical sites that showcase its illustrious past.

- Just a few of the historical locations that contribute to the city's vitality and architectural splendour include the renowned Belém Tower, the Jerónimos Monastery, and the So Jorge Castle.

Urban art

- Lisbon is a centre for street art, and the city's walls are covered in colourful murals and graffiti.

- The city's streets act as an outdoor gallery, displaying the creations of regional and international street artists and bringing a lively and vibrant touch to the cityscape.

Gastronomic delights

- Lisbon has a vibrant and alluring food scene that offers both traditional and modern cuisine.

- Lisbon's diverse cuisine is a feast for the senses, from seafood specialties to pastéis de nata (Portuguese custard pastries).

Events and Festivals:

- Lisbon organises a variety of festivals and events all year long that add to its vitality.

- There is always something going on in the city, enhancing its dynamic and active atmosphere, from the fun Santo António celebrations in June to music festivals like NOS Alive and the Lisbon Book Fair.

Coastal Promenade:

- The Tagus River waterfront of Lisbon is a bustling neighbourhood with cutting-edge buildings, hip bars, and eateries.

- The spacious promenade offers a lively backdrop for strolls, taking in breathtaking vistas, and soaking up the energetic vibe of the city.

Lisbon is an intriguing location due to its blend of historical allure, cultural wealth, and modern vibrancy.

Lisbon, the dynamic capital of Portugal, provides an amazing experience whether you're exploring its historic neighbourhoods, delighting in local food, immersing yourself in the arts, or just taking in the busy atmosphere.

Estoril: Glamour and Casinos

Near Cascais on the Portuguese Riviera, Estoril is famed for its glitzy vibe and world-class casinos. Here's why Estoril is frequently linked to glitz and gambling:

Casino in Estoril:

- The Estoril Casino, one of the biggest and oldest casinos in Europe, is located in Estoril.

- The casino has a long history and was a popular destination for international elites and European nobles in the middle of the 20th century.

- Slot machines, table games, and poker tournaments are just a few of the many gambling options available, making for an exciting and opulent gaming experience.

James Bond Relationship

- The James Bond book and movie "Casino Royale" further established Estoril's relationship with glitz and casinos.

- The casino at Estoril is portrayed in the narrative as a lavish venue for high-stakes gaming, enhancing its allure and renown around the world.

Beautiful architecture

- Estoril has beautiful architecture that pays homage to its opulent history.

- The terrain is dotted with opulent resorts, stately homes, and chic houses that exude sophistication and refinement.

Gourmet food and nightlife

- Estoril has a thriving dining and nightlife scene, with posh eateries, hip bars, and elegant clubs.

- Indulge in fine dining, take in live music, or enjoy the thrill of a stylish night out in Estoril.

Resorts and beaches:

- Estoril is located on a magnificent coastline and has lovely beaches.

- There are several upscale resorts and beach clubs in the area that offer opulent beachside experiences to visitors.

Events and Performances in the Arts:

- Concerts, plays, and art exhibits are just a few of the cultural activities that Estoril hosts all year long.

- These activities enhance the region's glitz and cultural diversity and draw tourists from all around the world.

Estoril is a popular travel destination for individuals looking for a taste of luxury and excitement because of its glitzy ambiance, lavish casinos, and attractive surroundings.

Estoril offers a spectacular experience that is certain to leave a lasting impression, whether you are drawn to the excitement of gambling, the appeal of exclusive eateries, or the elegance of the Riviera lifestyle.

Mafra: Palaces and the Countryside

Mafra, a delightful town in Portugal's Lisbon Region, is well-known for its grand palaces and lovely surroundings. Here's why Mafra is frequently connected to palaces and open spaces:

National Palace of Mafra:

- The beautiful Baroque palace complex known as the Mafra National Palace often referred to as the Palace-Convent of Mafra, towers over the city.

- One of Portugal's most important buildings, it has great architecture and a large interior that includes a beautiful church, royal apartments, a library, and a convent.

Mafra Basilica:

- A crucial component of the Mafra National Palace complex is the Basilica of Mafra.

- For lovers of art and architecture, this grand church is a must-see because of its opulent decorations, complex carvings, and magnificent pipe organ.

Mafra's Rural Area:

- Beyond the palace, Mafra is encircled by stunning terrain made up of undulating hills, breathtaking views, and sleepy rural communities.

- The countryside provides chances for strolls, cycling, and discovering the area's stunning natural surroundings.

National Tapada de Mafra

- The Mafra National Palace is located in the Tapada Nacional de Mafra, a sizable enclosed park and animal sanctuary.

- For those who enjoy nature, this protected region offers a serene and beautiful getaway with its various flora and wildlife.

Rural customs:

- The rural areas of Mafra are a reflection of conventional rural life and agricultural methods.

- Local customs can be seen by visitors, including farming operations, vineyards, and the creation of traditional goods like cheese, honey, and wine.

Cultural Festivals and Events:

- Mafra organises several festivals and cultural gatherings to honour regional cultures and traditions.

- Events that highlight the town's cultural heritage include the Feira do Livro de Mafra (Book Fair) and the yearly Festas do Concelho de Mafra.

Grand palaces, bucolic vistas, and cultural traditions combine to create a singular experience for visitors in Mafra.

Mafra offers a beautiful fusion of history, natural beauty, and traditional charm, whether you're touring the sumptuous Mafra National Palace, taking a stroll through the countryside, or participating in local celebrations.

Arrábida Natural Park

Near Lisbon, Portugal's capital city, on the Setbal Peninsula is the breathtaking natural preserve known as Arrábida Natural Park. It is well known for its gorgeous coastline landscape, immaculate beaches, and varied ecosystems. What makes Arrábida Natural Park a must-see location is listed below:

Coastal splendour

- A stunning coastline with towering limestone cliffs, undiscovered bays, and a blue sea can be found in Arrábida Natural Park.

- A gorgeous and dreamlike environment is created by the stark contrast between the deep blue sea and the bright foliage.

Beaches:

- The park is home to some of Portugal's most stunning beaches, with clean sands and serene waters.

- Stunning beaches where you can unwind, swim, and soak up the sun include Praia da Figueirinha, Praia do Portinho da Arrábida, and Praia dos Coelhos.

Nature's diversity and flora

- A haven for biodiversity, Arrábida Natural Park is home to a wide range of plant and animal species.

- The park is renowned for its Mediterranean vegetation, which includes cork oaks, stone pines, and fragrant bushes and creates a scented and colourful scene.

Marine life reserves and underwater parks:

- The Arrábida Natural Park's coastal waters are part of a marine protected area.

- The park's crystal-clear waters are home to a wide variety of marine life, making it a well-liked location for diving, snorkelling, and discovering sub aquatic ecosystems.

Nature trails and hiking trails

- A network of clearly marked hiking and nature paths in the park allows visitors to appreciate its scenic splendour on foot.

- These routes take you through verdant forests, along clifftop walkways, and offer breathtaking panoramic views of the nearby landscape.

The Convent of Arrabida

- Convento de Arrábida, a Franciscan monastery built in the sixteenth century and set atop a hill inside the park, is tucked away.

- The monastery provides a serene haven and a distinctive vantage point to take in the park's breathtaking vistas.

Outdoor Recreation

- Outdoor pursuits like birdwatching, mountain biking, and rock climbing are possible at the Arrábida Natural Park.

- Both nature lovers and those looking for adventure can play in the park's different natural environments.

Nature lovers, outdoor enthusiasts, and people seeking quiet in the middle of stunning beauty will find nirvana in Arrábida Natural Park. A trip to Arrábida Natural Park guarantees an exceptional experience and a close connection to nature's splendour, whether you're relaxing on the clean beaches, discovering the varied ecosystems, or going on outdoor adventures.

SHOPPING AND NIGHTLIFE

Cascais Shopping Center

Modern shopping centre Cascais Shopping Center, often known as CascaiShopping, is situated in Cascais, Portugal. It attracts both locals and tourists because of the wide variety of stores, boutiques, and entertainment opportunities it provides. What to expect when visiting Cascais Shopping Center is as follows:

Shopping Centers:

- The Cascais Shopping Center is home to a range of retail establishments, including local shops, multinational chains, and fashion boutiques.

- Explore the mall to find a variety of apparel, accessories, gadgets, household products, and other items.

Restaurants and food courts:

- The shopping complex has a food court with a selection of fast-food restaurants, sit-down restaurants, and international cuisines.

- There are standalone restaurants in the mall that offer a variety of cuisine options if you prefer a sit-down meal experience.

Supermarkets and quick-service restaurants

- A supermarket is part of the Cascais Shopping Center, where you can buy groceries, fresh vegetables, furniture, and other necessities.

- For your convenience, the mall also includes convenience stores and specialty merchants.

Amusement & leisure

- The shopping mall has entertainment alternatives available, including a movie theatre complex where you may watch the newest releases.

- The mall may also contain arcades, game rooms, or other leisure pursuits that amuse people of all ages.

Services:

- To meet your needs, Cascais Shopping Center provides a range of services, including financial establishments, ATMs, cell phone retailers, and beauty parlours.

Accessibility and parking
- The mall is easily accessible by automobile thanks to the retail centre's extensive parking spots for guests.

- Bus stops and train stations are close by, making public transportation a simple option as well.

A variety of demands and tastes are met by the full shopping experience offered by Cascais Shopping Center.

The mall provides a handy and wide range of options, whether you're looking for clothes, electronics, groceries, or a place to eat and unwind. While experiencing the dynamic city of Cascais, enjoy your shopping experience at the Cascais Shopping Center.

Mercado da Vila

In the centre of Cascais, Portugal, is a bustling market called Mercado da Vila, sometimes referred to as Cascais Market. It offers a distinctive shopping experience where locals and visitors may buy local specialties, fresh fruit, handicrafts, and more. What to expect when visiting Mercado da Vila is as follows:

Local products and fresh produce:

- The market is renowned for its extensive variety of fresh fruits, vegetables, fish, meats, and dairy goods.

- You may taste the flavours of the area by purchasing the best produce from nearby farmers and traders.

Specialty Dishes and Delights:

- A range of regional delicacies and traditional Portuguese goods are sold at the Mercado da Vila.

- Portuguese cuisine is represented by artisanal cheeses, cured meats, olive oil, honey, pastries, and other delicacies.

Seafood and Fish:

- Cascais is known for its fresh fish and seafood because it is a coastal town, and the market is an excellent spot to locate a large assortment.

- You can choose from a variety of fish and seafood alternatives, including both domestic and international species.

Restaurants and Cafés:

- Mercado da Vila has several eateries where you can take a break from shopping and eat or drink something energising.

- There are options available to suit all tastes and preferences, whether you're in the mood for a quick snack or a filling supper.

Artisans and handicrafts:

- The market offers a variety of handcrafted goods and one-of-a-kind souvenirs, as well as showcasing the craftsmanship of regional craftsmen.

- Handmade jewellery, ceramics, textiles, and other crafts may be found that make treasured presents or souvenirs.

Entertainment and Cultural Events:

- Cultural gatherings, live music performances, and other entertainment activities frequently take place at Mercado da Vila.

- These activities enhance the market's dynamic ambiance and give guests a colourful and pleasurable experience.

You can become fully immersed in the customs, tastes, and culture of Cascais by going to Mercado da Vila. It's a great spot to explore, sample local cuisine, and talk to helpful merchants.

Take advantage of the chance to taste seasonal fruit, find unusual goods, and take in the lively ambiance of this lively market in the centre of Cascais.

Artisan Crafts and Souvenirs

A wide range of artisanal goods are available in Cascais, including one-of-a-kind trinkets that showcase the area's rich cultural past and craftsmanship. You can find the following well-liked artisan goods and mementos in Cascais:

Ceramic and pottery:

- In Cascais, handcrafted ceramics and pottery are popular choices for souvenirs.

- Be on the lookout for exquisitely crafted vases, bowls, plates, and ornamental tiles that feature classic Portuguese patterns and motifs.

Cork-based goods

- Cascais provides a variety of cork goods that make for distinctive and environmentally friendly souvenirs. Portugal is well recognized for its cork manufacture.

- Look for accessories made of cork that showcase the material's inherent beauty and adaptability, such as bags, wallets, coasters, and other items.

Jewellery produced by hand:

- Another fantastic option for souvenirs that lets you bring home a piece of Portuguese artistry is artisan jewellery.

- Look for handcrafted jewellery such as rings, bracelets, earrings, and necklaces that use silver, filigree, or vibrant glass beads.

Embroidery and textiles:

- Portuguese embroidery and traditional fabrics are prized for their deft craftsmanship and beautiful motifs.

- Look for woven, tapestries, and embroidered fabrics that highlight the area's cultural past.

Souvenirs with a Sardine and Fish theme:

- Since it is a coastal community, Cascais is well renowned for its fishing heritage, and sardines are a common motif in regional trinkets.

- Look for products that honour this iconic figure in culture, such as sardine-shaped ceramic tiles, magnets, and keychains.

Portuguese-style ceramic tiles:

- Azulejos, or traditional Portuguese tiles, are a significant component of the nation's artistic legacy.

- Look for hand-painted tiles that may be displayed as decorative pieces or used as trivets and show elaborate patterns, historical scenes, or famous sites.

Local cuisine and wine

- Food and wine goods from Cascais are also well-known, making them excellent options for gifts.

- Think of bringing home regional wines, pastéis de nata (custard tarts), honey, preserves, and olive oil.

Search for stores, marketplaces, and boutiques in Cascais that specialise in handcrafted and regionally produced goods when looking for artisan crafts and souvenirs. To understand more about the products' histories and craftsmanship, interact with the vendors and artisans. You can support local craftsmen and bring a special piece of Cascais' cultural identity home by purchasing handcrafted goods as gifts.

Bars, Pubs, and Nightclubs

With a wide selection of bars, pubs, and nightclubs that accommodate all interests and preferences, Cascais has a thriving nightlife culture. Cascais has options to fit any mood, whether you're searching for a laid-back setting to have a drink, live music places, or energetic nightclubs. Here are a few well-known places to take into account:

The Guincho Bar

- Bar do Guincho, which is close to Guincho Beach, provides a relaxed beachfront atmosphere where you can unwind with a drink and take in the ocean views.

Pub. by John Bull

- John Bull Pub is a bustling British-style bar renowned for its welcoming environment, live sports broadcasts, and a variety of alcoholic beverages.

Inn at Chequers:

- In the heart of Cascais, Chequers Bar is a well-liked location with a warm and welcoming atmosphere.
- It offers a terrific location to unwind and mingle with live music, a fully

stocked bar, and occasionally DJ sessions.

Bar Jézebel Gin:

- Jézebel Gin Bar is a must-see if you're a gin enthusiast.

- It offers a wide variety of excellent gins and a welcoming setting ideal for sipping gin and tonics or trying inventive gin cocktails.

Club Tamariz Beach:

- In the nights, the beachside Tamariz Beach Club morphs into a buzzing nightlife.

- It's a popular option for people looking to dance the night away because it has a dance floor, a DJ spinning upbeat music, and an outside patio.

Cascais swing:

- A fashionable pub and nightclub with a chic atmosphere is called Swing Cascais.

- It offers a variety of musical genres, such as pop, hip-hop, and electronic music, and frequently hosts themed events and parties.

Estoril Casino:

- Although officially outside of Cascais, Casino Estoril is close by and provides a posh nightlife experience.

- It offers a variety of entertainment choices, such as betting, live performances, concerts, and themed events.

It's a good idea to research the opening times and any special events or performances scheduled for the night you intend to visit, as is the case with any nightlife scene.

Additionally, keep in mind to drink responsibly and follow any applicable admission restrictions or dress codes. Have a great night out in this energetic coastal town while visiting the broad array of bars, pubs, and nightclubs that Cascais has to offer.

Live Music and Entertainment

With numerous venues showcasing local and international talent in a variety of genres, Cascais has a thriving live music and entertainment scene. Cascais has lots to offer regardless of whether you enjoy live music, jazz, classical music, or cultural acts. Here are several locations in Cascais where you may see live music and entertainment:

Guia House:

- A picturesque cliffside complex called Casa da Guia is home to several bars and eateries, some of which provide live music performances.

- The relaxing and comfortable atmosphere is enhanced by enjoying a drink or meal while listening to live bands or solo artists.

Cultural Center of Cascais:

- Concerts, plays, dance performances, and other cultural events are frequently held in the Cascais Cultural Center.
- To learn about forthcoming concerts and become fully immersed in the

neighbourhood cultural scene, see the centre's schedule.

Area Pubs and Bars:

- On particular nights, Cascais has a lot of bars and pubs with live music.

- Live bands or acoustic performances are frequently featured at venues like John Bull Pub, Chequers Bar, or numerous eateries around Cascais Marina, creating a lively scene for music fans.

Events and Festivals:

- All through the year, Cascais holds several music festivals and events that include diverse genres and performers.

- If you want to know about any music festivals, jazz performances, or other cultural events happening while you're there, keep an eye on the neighbourhood event calendar.

Estoril Casino:

- Casino Estoril has a variety of entertainment alternatives, including live music performances, concerts, and shows, even though it is technically not in Cascais but close by.

- To see whether any musical or entertaining acts coincide with your visit, check their itinerary.

Festivals of Culture:

- The city of Cascais is well recognized for its cultural festivals, many of which include live music.

- One of the main festivals where you can take in live music concerts and performances by famous singers is the Festas do Mar, which takes place in August.

It is advised to check the timetables of the individual venues and the local event listings when making plans to take in live entertainment in Cascais to make sure you don't miss any shows.

Cascais offers a wide variety of options to please music lovers and those looking for entertainment, whether you're looking for a vibrant music scene or a more private setting to take in live performances.

PRACTICAL INFORMATION

Money and Currency Exchange

The Euro (€) is the designated currency of Cascais, Portugal. Information on money and currency exchange in Cascais is provided below:

Change of Currencies:

- Banks, currency exchange offices, and several hotels are just a few of the places in Cascais that offer currency exchange services.

- Before making a purchase, it is a good idea to compare exchange rates and transaction costs to be sure you are getting the best deal possible.

- Bring a legitimate form of identification with you, as you might be asked for one when exchanging money.

ATMs:

- In Cascais, there are several ATMs, and most of them accept popular international debit and credit cards.

- It's easy to get cash in the local currency by using ATMs.

- When using ATMs abroad, inquire with your bank about any possible fees or international transaction costs.

Charge cards:

- Most businesses in Cascais, including hotels, restaurants, shops, and larger retailers, accept credit cards, especially Visa and Mastercard.

- Smaller companies or locally focused organisations could prefer cash payments or impose a minimum purchase amount for card payments.

- Always keep extra cash on hand for smaller purchases or in case you come across locations that don't accept cards.

Checks for Travel:

- Traveler's checks are less frequently used these days, so it could be difficult to find locations in Cascais that accept them.

- For convenience and flexibility, it is advised to have a variety of payment options, including cash and cards.

Security and Safety:

- Although Cascais is a generally safe place to visit, it's necessary to use caution when handling money.

- When using an ATM, be aware of your surroundings, and keep big amounts of cash hidden from view.

- While travelling, it's a good idea to keep your cash, credit cards, and identification papers safe.

It's a good idea to tell your bank or credit card company about your trip before going to Cascais to make sure your cards will function there and to find out if there will be any penalties or restrictions. Furthermore, arriving with a small sum of local currency can help cover immediate costs like transportation or little purchases.

Local Language and Useful Phrases

Portuguese is the nation's official language, and Cascais is where most people speak it. Even though English is widely spoken in the Cascais tourism industry, attempting to communicate in the native tongue is always welcomed.

Following are some helpful Portuguese expressions that you may find useful while visiting Cascais:

- Hello - Olá (oh-LAH)
- Good morning - Bom dia (bohm DEE-ah)
- Good afternoon - Boa tarde (boh-ah TAR-deh)
- Good evening - Boa noite (boh-ah NOY-teh)
- Please - Por favor (por fah-VOHR)
- Thank you - Obrigado (oh-bree-GAH-doh) - for men, or

Obrigada (oh-bree-GAH-dah) - for women

- You're welcome - De nada (deh NAH-dah)
- Excuse me - Com licença (kohm lee-SEN-sah)
- Yes - Sim (seem)
- No - Não (now)
- Sorry - Desculpe (dehs-KOOL-peh)
- I don't understand - Não entendo (now en-TEN-doh)
- Do you speak English? - Fala inglês? (FAH-lah een-GLAYSH?)
- Where is...? - Onde fica...? (OHN-dee FEE-kah...?)
- How much does it cost? - Quanto custa? (KWAHN-toh KOOSH-tah?)
- Can you help me? - Pode me ajudar? (POH-deh meh ah-ju-DAR?)
- I would like... - Eu gostaria de... (eh-oo gohs-TAH-ree-ah deh...)
- Cheers! - Saúde! (sow-OO-deh)

- Where is the bathroom? - Onde fica o banheiro? (OHN-dee FEE-kah oh bahn-YAY-roh?)
- I'm sorry, I don't speak Portuguese well - Desculpe, não falo bem português (dehs-KOOL-peh, now FAH-loh bem por-too-GAYS)

Remember that showing respect and engaging with the local culture in Cascais can be achieved by attempting to speak a few simple Portuguese words. Even if the locals turn to English to assist you, they will respect your efforts.

Internet and Communication

Being a sophisticated and welcoming tourist location, Cascais provides visitors with decent internet connectivity and a range of communication alternatives. Here are some details regarding communication and the Internet in Cascais:

Access to Mobile Networks:

- You may use your mobile phone to stay connected in Cascais thanks to the city's strong mobile network coverage.

- MEO, Vodafone, and NOS, three significant network providers in Portugal, provide reliable coverage and data plans for both local and foreign visitors.

- Ask your carrier about the alternatives and charges for international roaming if you intend to use your mobile device in Cascais.

Wi-Fi accessibility

- Customers in many hotels, eateries, cafes, and public spaces in Cascais have access to free Wi-Fi.

- Popular tourist destinations frequently provide Wi-Fi hotspots where you may use your smartphone, tablet, or laptop to access the internet.

Online cafés:

- There are internet cafés in Cascais where you may use their computers and access the internet for a fee if you don't have access to the internet while travelling or prefer utilising a computer.

Messages and Calls:

- Check your mobile phone plan to make sure you have access to international calling and messaging if you need to make calls or send texts while visiting Cascais.

- To make calls and send messages via the internet, often at a lesser cost, think about using messaging apps like WhatsApp, Viber, or Skype.

Payphones in Public:

- There may still be a few public pay phones in some parts of Cascais, even though they are not as prevalent as they once were.

- Coins or prepaid calling cards, which may be bought at convenience stores or kiosks, are typically accepted.

Mailing Services

- Visit the neighbourhood post office, or "Correios," to buy stamps and send packages or postcards if you need to send mail or postcards from Cascais.

Services for Emergencies:

- The universal emergency number in Portugal is 112. Dial this number to get police, fire, or medical assistance.

If you anticipate using a lot of data or calling while visiting Cascais, make sure your smartphone is compatible with the area's network and think about buying a local SIM card.

It should be simple and convenient to stay connected and communicate with others in Cascais given the availability of internet connections and a variety of communication channels.

Medical Services and Pharmacies

To meet the healthcare needs of locals and visitors, Cascais offers reputable medical services and fully-stocked pharmacies. Here is some information on Cascais's pharmacies and medical facilities:

Centres for public health:

- The "Centro de Sade" public health centres in Cascais are places where you can go for non-emergency medical care.

- These clinics offer primary healthcare, general medical consultations, and immunizations.

- If you need medical care, get in touch with your neighbourhood health centre to learn more about their offerings and appointment availability.

Private medical facilities:

- Private medical facilities in Cascais provide a greater range of healthcare services, including specialised consultations, diagnostic procedures, and emergency care.

- These institutions typically demand payment for services rendered or health insurance coverage.

- It is a good idea to obtain travel insurance that will pay for any medical emergency you may encounter while visiting Cascais.

Pharmacies:

- In Cascais, pharmacies, or "Farmácias," are readily available.

- They provide prescription drugs, over-the-counter medicines, and fundamental medical supplies.

- Although most pharmacies are open during standard business hours, you can discover those that operate on a rotating 24-hour basis and are referred to as "Farmácias de Serviço."

Medications on prescription:

- During your visit to Cascais, if you require a prescription medication refill, stop by a drugstore and show the pharmacist your prescription.

- It's best to bring along an appropriate quantity of vital drugs because some may not be available or have different brand names than in your home country.

Emergencies in Medicine:

- For rapid assistance in a medical emergency, use the 112 emergency hotline throughout Europe.

- The operator will send the necessary emergency assistance, such as an ambulance, to your area.

It is advised to carry the required contact information for your insurance provider and to have travel insurance that covers medical emergencies.

Additionally, get acquainted with the closest pharmacies and medical facilities around your lodging in case you encounter any unanticipated medical needs while visiting Cascais.

Tips for Sustainable Tourism

For a resort like Cascais to maintain its ecological, cultural, and social components, sustainable tourism is crucial. Here are some ideas to encourage eco-friendly tourist behaviours while you're there:

Environment Respect:

- In Cascais, be aware of your surroundings. Avoid leaving behind litter, and properly dispose of waste in designated bins.

- By taking shorter showers, shutting off lights and electronics when not in use, and reusing towels and bedsheets in your lodging, you can save water and energy.

Supporting regional companies:

- To help the neighbourhood's economy and community, choose to stay at locally-owned hotels and eat at locally-owned restaurants.

- Choose locally sourced goods and services to support local businesses and lessen your carbon footprint.

Participate in Proactive Activities:

- Take part in events and excursions that have an emphasis on protecting the environment and culture.

- Avoid engaging in activities that harm the environment or exploit animals.

- When visiting Cascais, opt for environmentally friendly modes of transportation like walking, cycling, or taking the bus or train.

Respect for regional customs and culture:

- Respect the local traditions and cultural standards of Cascais by learning about them before your trip.

- When visiting religious or cultural sites, dress accordingly.

- Respectfully converse with locals and be eager to discover their customs and way of life.

Reduce Plastic Use

- To decrease the consumption of single-use plastics, carry a reusable water bottle and fill it up at water fountains or from taps.

- When visiting markets or stores, remember to bring your reusable shopping bags.

Natural resource preservation

- Be responsible when admiring Cascais's natural beauty. Keep to authorised pathways, don't harm plants and animals, and don't disturb wildlife.

- If there are any available during your visit, think about taking part in local conservation efforts or beach clean-ups.

Education for Both You and Others

- Learn about the issues affecting Cascais' ecology and culture as well as its efforts to be sustainable.

- Discuss responsible tourism with other travellers and spread the word about it.

You can maintain Cascais's natural beauty, assist the neighbourhood, and help to preserve its cultural history for future generations by implementing these sustainable tourist practices.

Useful Contacts and Resources

It's beneficial to have access to helpful contacts and resources while you're in Cascais. The following are some crucial numbers and resources that can help you during your stay:

Services for Emergencies:

- Emergency (Fire, Medical, Police): 112 Local Governments:

- Municipality of Cascais: (351) 21 481, 50 00 Tourist Information:

- Tourism Office in Cascais: +351 21 481 37 30
- Website for Cascais: www.visitcascais.com

Medicinal Facilities and Hospitals:

- Cascais Hospital: +351 21 482 77 00
- Embassy or Consulate: Centro de Saúde de Cascais (Health Center): +351 21 482 72 50

Consular assistance may be obtained at your country's embassy or consulate in Lisbon. Transportation:

- Information about trains and buses is available at www.scotturb.com and www.cp.pt/en.

- Taxi Service in Cascais: +351 21 483 01 35

Expired or Stolen Credit Cards:

- To report any lost or stolen cards, get in touch with your credit card company right away.

Banking services and foreign exchange:

- Information and services for currency exchange and banking needs can be obtained from nearby banks and currency exchange offices.

Weather Prediction:

- Check the Cascais, Portugal, weather forecast before you go out and make any plans.

Travel Protection:

- For assistance with medical crises, travel delays, or other covered situations, get in touch with your travel insurance provider.

It's advised to store these crucial contacts in your phone or keep them nearby while you're there. In case of crises, it's also a good idea to have a hard copy or digital copy of your passport, travel insurance, and other important documents. Enjoy your time seeing the lovely city of Cascais while remaining informed and prepared.

Printed in Great Britain
by Amazon

26319650R00109